# RECIPES
*from the*
# VINEYARDS
*of*
# NORTHERN CALIFORNIA

# Appetizers

*Leslie Mansfield*

**CELESTIALARTS**
*Berkeley, California*

*When preparing recipes that call for egg yolks or whites, whether or not they are to be cooked, use only the highest quality, salmonella-free eggs.*

## CELESTIALARTS

P.O. Box 7123
Berkeley, California 94707

Distributed in Canada by Ten Speed Canada, in the United Kingdom and Europe by Airlift Books, in New Zealand by Southern Publishers Group, in Australia by Simon & Schuster Australia, in South Africa by Real Books, and in Singapore, Malaysia, Hong Kong, and Thailand by Berkeley Books.

Cover and interior design by Greene Design
Cover photograph by Larry Kunkel
Photo styling by Veronica Randall
Public Domain Art thanks to Dover Publications

Library of Congress Card Catalog Number 99-70629

First printing, 1999
Printed in the United States

1 2 3 4 5 6 7—03 02 01 00 99

*Dedicated to the memory of*
*DAVID HINDS,*
*with deepest gratitude for taking a chance on me.*

## ACKNOWLEDGMENTS

*Deepest gratitude goes to my husband Richard, who has helped me with every step—his name belongs on the title page along with mine. To my wonderful parents, Stewart and Marcia Whipple, for their unflagging confidence. To my editor Veronica Randall, who is everything I could ever want in a friend. To my editor Heather Garnos, who helps keep it all together. To Brad Greene, for another spectacular design. To Larry Kunkel, for his glorious photography.*

*Finally, this book would not have been possible without the cooperation of the many people at the wineries who graciously contributed their favorite recipes. I wish to thank them all for their generosity.*

# *Table of Contents*

# *Introduction*

Just mention California wine country and thoughts of warm sunshine, vines heavy with ripening grapes, and a relaxed lifestyle come to mind. The small villages throughout the wine country each have their own personalities, as do the wineries. From rural family-run boutique wineries to large, stately wineries surrounded by a sea of vineyards, they all have one thing in common—a love for good food and wine.

This love of food and wine has resulted in an explosion of cutting-edge ideas that have defined California cuisine, incorporating the finest of Europe and Asia while drawing on the incredible local and seasonal bounty.

Entertaining is a way of life in wine country. Whether it is a formal dinner with many courses to showcase a variety of wines, or just drawing off a pitcher of new wine from the barrel to go with an impromptu picnic with neighbors, the desire to share the best they have to offer has helped shape the cuisine of California.

In the following pages you will find recipes offered from the finest wineries of northern California. Each is a reflection of their personality, whether formal or casual, and all are delicious. Each one is a taste of wine country.

*1*

## HANDLEY CELLARS

*Known as much for exquisite sparkling wines as for superbly crafted still wines, Milla Handley practices her craft at the cellars she and her husband Rex McClellan founded in 1975. Set in the northwest end of the Anderson Valley, protected to the west by redwood-covered coastal ridges and to the east by oak-studded hills, Handley Cellars is situated in a unique viticultural region. The Mendocino appellation, by virtue of its cool foggy nights and gentle summers, is ideally suited to the production of aromatic and delicate whites, luscious and elegant reds, and crisp and flavorful sparklers.*

# CARIBBEAN CRAB DIP

*Habanero sauce is made from the hottest chile known, so go easy — you don't want to overpower the rest of the flavors.*

4 ounces cream cheese

1/2 cup unsweetened coconut milk

Juice of 2 limes

1/2 teaspoon salt

1 pound crab meat, picked over for shells

1 red bell pepper, finely diced

2 scallions, finely diced

Habanero sauce to taste

In a large bowl, blend cream cheese, coconut milk, lime juice, and salt until smooth. Stir in crab meat, bell pepper, and scallions until well mixed. Add the habanero sauce, a few drops at a time, until desired heat is reached. Serve with crackers or raw vegetables.

*Makes about 3 cups*
*Serve with Handley Cellars*
*Dry Creek Valley Chardonnay*

## TOAD HOLLOW
## VINEYARDS

*Todd Williams (Dr. Toad) and his reclusive winemaker, known only as the dancing badger on Toad Hollow's label, have fashioned Toad Hollow with a commitment to producing the highest quality wine at the most affordable price. They purposefully choose not to age their Chardonnay in oak, preferring instead to maintain the delicate fruit of their grapes by cool-fermenting in 100 percent stainless steel. After yeast and subsequent malolactic fermentation, their wines are fruity and refreshing, without the distraction of big, bold wood. Toadmaster Todd also produces a delicate rosé from a blend of Pinot Noir and Petite Sirah. Their name for it? What else but Eye of the Toad. When asked about his wine priorities, Dr. Toad summarizes them succinctly, "Enjoy it with pleasure, enjoy it often, and don't make a big deal out of it."*

# ARTICHOKE &
SALMON DIP

*This is an excellent and easy dip for
casual afternoon get-togethers. It's also a
great way to use up leftover salmon.*

6 ounces cooked salmon, flaked

1 (14-ounce) can artichoke bottoms in water,
    drained and chopped

1 (6-ounce) jar marinated artichoke hearts,
    drained and chopped

1 (4-ounce) can green chiles, drained
    and chopped

1 cup grated Parmesan cheese

1 cup mayonnaise

2 cloves garlic, minced

1/2 teaspoon Tabasco

1/2 teaspoon freshly ground black pepper

Preheat oven to 350° F. Lightly oil a 1 1/2-quart
baking dish.

In the bowl of a food processor, combine all
ingredients. Process until smooth, scraping sides
often. Place mixture in prepared baking dish. Bake
for about 35 minutes, or until hot and bubbly. Serve
with sliced baguettes, crackers, or raw vegetables.

*Makes about 2 cups*
*Serve with Toad Hollow Chardonnay*

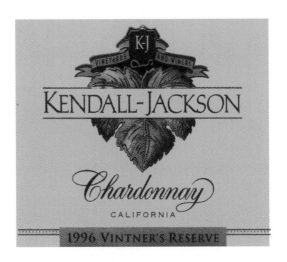

## KENDALL-JACKSON
## WINERY

*In 1974, Jess Jackson and his family purchased an 85-acre pear ranch near Lakeport in northern California. By 1982, the ranch was a vineyard, the barn was a tasting room, and the pasture was a winery. Meanwhile, they studied the premium vineyards that span California's cool coastal growing regions and discovered the wonderful spectrum of flavors produced by the same grape varietal grown in different locations. Why not use this exciting diversity? Why not blend the best grapes from the best vineyards to produce unique wines with layers of depth and complexity? Their first Chardonnay was made in 1982, from vineyards in Santa Barbara, Monterey, Sonoma, and Lake Counties. This wine was named "Best American Chardonnay" by the American Wine Competition. Their concept of blending the best with the best was affirmed and to this day continues to be the reason their wines are noted for their consistency and complexity, vintage after vintage.*

# ROMESCO DIP

*Couple this with a bowl of cured olives and thinly sliced dried salami for an alfresco lunch when good friends drop by.*

4 red bell peppers, halved lengthwise
    and seeded

3 tablespoons olive oil

1/3 cup chopped almonds, lightly toasted

1/4 cup finely chopped dill pickles

1/4 cup Kendall-Jackson Cabernet Sauvignon

Juice of 1 lemon

1 tablespoon balsamic vinegar

1 tablespoon olive oil

Salt and freshly ground black pepper

Preheat oven to 450° F. Lightly oil a rimmed baking sheet.

Place bell peppers, skin-side-up, on prepared baking sheet. Drizzle with 3 tablespoons olive oil. Roast for about 20 minutes, or until peppers are charred all over. Remove from oven and immediately place peppers in a bowl and cover with plastic wrap. Let stand for 15 minutes. When cool enough to handle, slip off skins and discard.

*(recipe continued on next page)*

In the bowl of a food processor, process toasted almonds until finely ground. Add roasted peppers and process until smooth. With a flexible spatula, scrape mixture into a bowl. Add pickles, wine, lemon juice, vinegar, and 1 tablespoon olive oil and stir to mix well. Season with salt and pepper. Cover and chill for at least 1 hour to allow flavors to marry. Serve with toasted baguette slices.

*Makes approximately 2 cups*
*Serve with Kendall-Jackson*
*Cabernet Sauvignon*

*Good wine is a good familiar creature if it be well used.*

**Shakespeare**

CHARDONNAY

SONOMA COUNTY

1 9 9 7

ALC. 13.8% BY VOL.

## SEBASTIANI VINEYARDS

*In the late 1800s, Samuele Sebastiani—working with a horse-drawn wagon, an antique crusher, a basket press, and a 500-gallon redwood tank—founded the winery that bears his name. Samuele was born with a dogged determination and a will to succeed, and out of those humble beginnings grew a winery that was to become the fourth largest in the United States. Samuele's son August and August's wife Sylvia purchased the winery in 1952, and were instrumental in introducing new ideas. From the bottling of popularly priced magnums, to creating the blush wine category with the Eye of the Swan Pinot Noir Blanc, August and Sylvia have led the industry. Today, the third generation is continuing the Sebastiani tradition of quality and value while introducing premium and super-premium wines that are of the absolute highest quality. As Don Sebastiani says with pride, "Excellence in winemaking is a goal we have achieved."*

# ARTICHOKE FRITTATA SQUARES

*These mouth-watering treats are reminiscent of a hearty quiche. Serve them along with a glass of chilled Chardonnay when your guests first arrive. They are the perfect prelude to an Italian supper.*

3 (6-ounce) jars marinated artichoke hearts

3 bunches scallions, chopped

1 clove garlic, minced

8 eggs

10 soda crackers, crumbled

1 pound sharp Cheddar cheese, grated

1 cup Italian parsley leaves, finely chopped

1/4 teaspoon Tabasco

1/4 teaspoon Worcestershire sauce

1/2 teaspoon salt

1/2 teaspoon freshly ground black pepper

Preheat oven to 325° F. Lightly oil a 13 x 9-inch baking dish.

Drain artichoke hearts and reserve marinade. Chop artichoke hearts and set aside. In a skillet, heat artichoke marinade over medium heat. Add scallions and garlic and sauté until tender.

In a large bowl, whisk eggs until smooth. Add cracker crumbs and whisk until blended. Stir in artichoke hearts, cheese, parsley, Tabasco, Worcestershire sauce, salt, and pepper. Stir in scallion mixture until well blended. Pour into prepared baking dish. Bake for about 35 minutes, or until firm and light golden brown. Let cool. Cut into squares.

*Makes about 36 squares*
*Serve with Sebastiani Vineyards*
*Chardonnay*

## HOP KILN WINERY

*The Hop Kiln is one of the most famous landmarks in Sonoma County. On the register of National Historic Trust Buildings, the Kiln, which was built around the turn of the century, has been the backdrop for four movies and now houses a fine, well-respected Sonoma County winery. Renovated by Dr. Martin Griffin in the mid-sixties, it celebrated its first crush in 1974. The winery is now the home to sixty-five acres of wine grapes that include Chardonnay, Gewürztraminer, Cabernet Sauvignon, and Valdiguié.*

# APRICOT
# BAKED BRIE

*The flavors of the apricots are mirrored
beautifully by the aromatic fruit of
Hop Kiln's Johannisberg Riesling.
The Johannisberg Riesling is also known
as the White Riesling.*

1 cup diced canned apricots, drained

1 cup Hop Kiln Winery Johannisberg Riesling

1-pound Brie wheel, rind trimmed

1/3 cup sliced almonds, lightly toasted

Preheat oven to 350° F. Lightly oil a pie plate.

In a saucepan, stir together apricots and wine.
Bring to a simmer over medium heat and simmer
until liquid is reduced to about 1/4 cup. Place Brie
in prepared pie plate and pour apricot mixture over
the top. Sprinkle almonds over the top. Bake for
about 15 minutes, or until hot and bubbly. Serve
with crackers or sliced baguettes.

*Serves 6 to 8
Serve with Hop Kiln Winery
Johannisberg Riesling*

## TURNBULL
## WINE CELLARS

*Just south of Oakville in the Napa Valley, Patrick O'Dell, proprietor of Turnbull Wine Cellars, produces stunning wines of amazing complexity and depth. His well-known red wines include Cabernet Sauvignon, Merlot, and Sangiovese, as well as small amounts of Syrah and Zinfandel. A limited amount of elegant Sauvignon Blanc is a special treat for white-wine lovers who visit his tasting room.*

# AUTUMN FIGS
## *Filled with Goat Cheese & Tarragon*

*Beverley Wolfe, Turnbull Wine Cellars' Executive Chef, created this sweet, savory starter.*

3 ounces walnuts, chopped

6 ounces soft goat cheese, crumbled

3 tablespoons heavy cream

1 tablespoon minced fresh tarragon

Salt and freshly ground black pepper

24 ripe figs, cut in half lengthwise

Chopped fresh tarragon, for garnish

Preheat oven to 350°F.

Place walnuts on a baking sheet. Bake for about 5 minutes, or until lightly toasted. Let cool.

In a bowl, blend together goat cheese, cream, tarragon, salt, and pepper until smooth. Put mixture in a pastry bag fitted with a star tip. Pipe about 1 teaspoon into the center of each fig half. Gently press walnuts into the cheese mixture. Sprinkle with additional tarragon to garnish.

*Makes 48 hors d'oeuvres*
*Serve with Turnbull Wine Cellars*
*Sangiovese*

## STONEGATE WINERY

*Steep slopes, shallow, stony loam soil, and excellent drainage force the vines in Stonegate's vineyards to compete intensely with each other. The results are clearly visible in the reds from these vineyards. Cabernet Sauvignon, Merlot, and Cabernet Franc exhibit excellent structure, dark color, and long, lingering finishes. At their best when paired with a fine meal, the wines are full of nuance and flavor. The Chardonnay, planted at the extreme north end of the Napa Valley in the hillside Bella Vista Vineyard, is multilayered and chock-full of ripe fruit aromas. Stonegate's Estate Bottled Sauvignon Blanc and Late Harvest Dessert Wine come from the vineyard surrounding the winery.*

# CROSTINI *with* *Olives & Mushrooms*

*Be sure to enjoy them with a glass of crisp*
*Sauvignon Blanc.*

2 tablespoons butter

8 ounces mushrooms, chopped

1/4 cup Italian parsley leaves, minced

2 cloves garlic, minced

2 tablespoons Stonegate Winery Sauvignon Blanc

8 ounces pitted Kalamata olives

3 tablespoons olive oil

Baguette slices, toasted

In a skillet, melt butter over medium heat. Add mushrooms, parsley, and garlic and sauté until mushrooms are tender. Add wine and sauté until liquid has evaporated. Let cool. In the bowl of a food processor, combine mushroom mixture and olives and process until chopped, scraping sides of the bowl often. With the motor running, add the olive oil and process until well combined. Spread the mixture thinly on the toasted baguettes.

*Makes about 1 1/2 cups*
*Serve with Stonegate Winery*
*Sauvignon Blanc*

ORGANICALLY GROWN GRAPES

## Mont St. John

1996 CARNEROS • ESTATE BOTTLED
### CHARDONNAY

ALCOHOL 13.8% BY VOLUME

## MONT ST. JOHN
## CELLARS

*A respect for the land and family traditions are traits that characterize owner and winemaker Andrea "Buck" Bartolucci. One of the first to recognize the uniqueness of the Carneros district, Buck, together with his father Louis, purchased and planted 160 acres of Pinot Noir and Chardonnay. Following early success with their grapes, Buck and Louis purchased a small plot of land in 1977 near their vineyards and started Mont St. John Cellars. Buck, as president and winemaker, believes that the vineyard should always dictate the style of the wine. Although he has a degree in enology and viticulture, he considers himself a caretaker, rather than a viticulturist; this unique attitude shows in the quality of his wines.*

# STUFFED MUSHROOMS

*These will disappear as fast as you can serve them, so play it safe and double the batch.*

1 pound large mushrooms (about 20)

1 cup Italian seasoned breadcrumbs

1/4 cup minced red onion

1/4 cup melted butter

1/2 cup freshly grated Parmesan cheese

Preheat oven to 350° F. Lightly oil an 8 x 8-inch baking dish.

Remove stems from mushrooms and place caps into the prepared baking dish. Finely chop the stems and place in a bowl. Add breadcrumbs and onion and stir to mix. Stir in butter until mixture is evenly moistened. With a small spoon, fill mushroom caps with breadcrumb mixture. Sprinkle Parmesan cheese over the top. Bake for about 20 minutes, or until golden brown. Serve immediately.

*Makes 20 hors d'oeuvres*
*Serve with Mont St. John Cellars*
*Chardonnay*

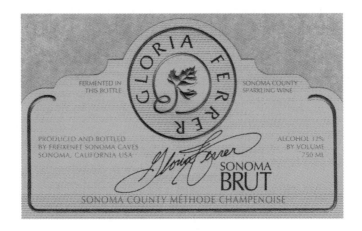

## GLORIA FERRER
## CHAMPAGNE CAVES

*Founded by José Ferrer, son of Pedro Ferrer Bosch, the Spanish-Catalan founder of Freixenet, Gloria Ferrer Champagne Caves was opened to the public in July of 1986. Named for José Ferrer's beloved wife, Gloria, the winery has been winning awards and the accolades of wine critics ever since. Located within the cool Carneros appellation, the beautiful building with stucco walls, arched windows, and overhanging balconies is a piece of the proud history of old Spain.*

# MUSHROOMS
# À LA GLORIA

*These delicate mushrooms would be
a welcome addition to a champagne buffet.*

3 tablespoons butter

1 tablespoon minced garlic

1$^1$/2 pounds mushrooms, stems removed
and discarded

1$^1$/2 cups Gloria Ferrer Brut

3 tablespoons cold butter, cut into small pieces

Salt and freshly ground black pepper

2 tablespoons minced parsley

In a large skillet, melt 3 tablespoons of the butter over medium heat. Add garlic and sauté until fragrant. Add mushrooms and cook until lightly browned on both sides. Stir in wine and simmer until liquid is reduced to about $^1$/3 cup. Remove from heat and, with a slotted spoon, place mushrooms in a serving dish and keep warm. Whisk cold butter into the skillet, a little at a time, until all of the butter is incorporated. Season sauce with salt and pepper. Pour sauce over mushrooms and sprinkle with parsley.

*Serves 6*
*Serve with Gloria Ferrer Brut*

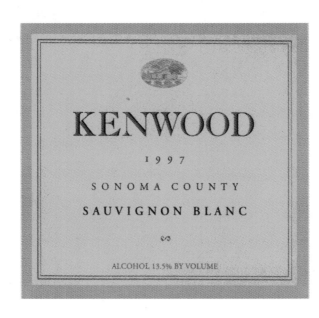

## KENWOOD VINEYARDS

*At Kenwood Vineyards, each vineyard lot is handled separately within the winery to preserve its individuality. Such "small lot" winemaking allows the winemaker to bring each lot of wine to its fullest potential. This style of winemaking is evident in the quality of Kenwood's special bottlings. From the Jack London Vineyard series, whose grapes come from the historical lava-terraced vineyards of the Jack London Ranch, to the Artist Series Cabernet Sauvignon, whose labels each year feature the work of a renowned artist, Kenwood's reds show Sonoma at its best.*

# PEAR & BRIE QUESADILLA

*Kenwood's executive chef Linda Kittler came up with these quick and easy appetizers. For the best flavor and texture, serve them while they're still hot.*

2 (10-inch) flour tortillas

1 pear, cut into 16 slices

1/4 cup finely chopped red onion

1 pound Brie, cut into 1/4-inch slices

1/2 teaspoon minced serrano chile

1/2 teaspoon salt

Preheat oven to 450° F. Lightly oil a baking sheet. Place tortillas on prepared baking sheet. Divide pear slices and red onion on top. Place Brie slices evenly on top. Sprinkle with chile and salt. Place in hot oven and bake for about 3 to 5 minutes, or until edges of tortilla are browned and cheese is melted. Remove from oven and let sit for 3 minutes. Cut each quesadilla into 8 wedges.

*Serves 6 to 8*
*Serve with Kenwood Vineyards and Winery*
*Sonoma County Sauvignon Blanc*

## SUTTER HOME
## WINERY

*Sutter Home is one of California's enviable success stories. Begun in 1874, the winery passed into the hands of its current family-owners in 1947, when John and Mario Trinchero immigrated from Italy and set down roots in the Napa Valley. Today their children carry on this once mom-and-pop operation. A milestone occurred in 1972 when, in an effort to make his red Zinfandel more robust, Bob Trinchero drew off some of the free run juice and fermented it as a "white" wine. This pale pink wine became a favorite at the winery's tasting room, and thus was born White Zinfandel. Today Sutter Home is known not only for this invention, but also for their high-quality, affordable varietal wines and their line of nonalcoholic wines.*

# QUESADILLAS *with Mushrooms, Goat Cheese, Pine Nuts & Herbs*

*Jeffrey Starr, Sutter Home's executive chef, took a Latin American classic and drew upon the best of California's local ingredients and came up with these tasty appetizers.*

1 tablespoon butter

1 tablespoon olive oil

6 ounces fresh shiitake mushrooms, thinly sliced

2 cloves garlic, minced

1 scallion, minced

2 tablespoons minced cilantro

4 (8-inch) flour tortillas

4 ounces soft goat cheese, crumbled

1 cup grated Monterey Jack pepper cheese

2 tablespoons pine nuts, lightly toasted

Preheat oven to 350° F. Lightly oil a baking sheet.

*(recipe continued on next page)*

In a skillet, melt the butter and olive oil together over medium heat. Add the mushrooms and sauté until tender. Add the garlic, scallion, and cilantro and sauté until liquid has evaporated. Set aside.

Place 2 tortillas on a baking sheet. Divide the goat cheese evenly between the two tortillas. Divide the mushroom mixture over the goat cheese. Sprinkle one-quarter of the Monterey Jack over each tortilla. Sprinkle the pine nuts over the top. Divide the remaining Monterey Jack over the top. Place remaining tortillas on top and press gently. Bake for about 10 minutes, or until cheese is just melted. Cut into 6 wedges.

*Serves 4 to 6*
*Serve with Sutter Home Winery*
*White Zinfandel*

## KORBEL CHAMPAGNE
## CELLARS

*Located just east of Guerneville and just a handful of miles inland from the Pacific Ocean, Korbel Champagne Cellars is a name that has stood for fine méthode-champenoise sparkling wines for over a hundred years. Founded in the late 1880s by three immigrant brothers from Bohemia—Francis, Anton, and Joseph Korbel—and owned and managed by the Heck family since 1954, Korbel has developed into one of California's most respected champagne houses.*

# CRAB & AVOCADO QUESADILLAS
## *with Mango Salsa*

*Chef Phil McGauley created a special crab guacamole to fill these festive quesadillas.*

**MANGO SALSA:**

1 mango, peeled and diced

2 Roma tomatoes, seeded and diced

2 scallions, chopped

Juice of 1 lime

1 tablespoon minced fresh mint

1 tablespoon raspberry vinegar

Salt and freshly ground black pepper


**CRAB AND AVOCADO QUESADILLAS:**

1 1/2 cups cooked crab meat, shredded

6 ounces Monterey Jack pepper cheese, shredded

1 avocado, diced

1/2 cup chopped scallions

1/3 cup chopped cilantro

1/4 cup chopped roasted red bell pepper

2 tablespoons freshly squeezed lime juice

Salt and freshly ground black pepper

6 (8-inch) flour tortillas

**For the salsa:** In a bowl, combine all ingredients and toss gently. Cover and chill at least 1 hour to allow flavors to develop.

**For the quesadillas:** Preheat oven to 350° F. Lightly oil a baking sheet. In a bowl, combine crab meat, cheese, avocado, scallions, cilantro, bell pepper, and lime juice and toss gently to mix. Season with salt and pepper to taste. Place 3 tortillas on prepared baking sheet. Divide the crab mixture on top of the tortillas and spread evenly. Top with remaining tortillas. Bake for about 10 minutes, or until the cheese is just melted. Cut each quesadilla into 6 triangles. Serve topped with mango salsa.

*Serves 6*
*Serve with Korbel Champagne Cellars*
*Natural Champagne*

## SHAFER VINEYARDS

*Located in the heart of the Stags Leap District of the Napa Valley, Shafer Vineyards has become synonymous with the finest the Napa Valley has to offer. Since their first crush in 1978, John Shafer and his son Doug have presided over the slow but steady growth of their premium winery, from the first 1000-case production to its present size. Highly acclaimed by colleagues within the wine industry, the wines from Shafer Vineyards reflect their terroir through their complex spectrum of aromas and flavors.*

# SAVORY TART *with Caramelized Onions, Gorgonzola & Walnuts*

*The flavors of this tart work together in beautiful unison. Serve hot out of the oven.*

**PASTRY:**

1 1/2 cups all-purpose flour

2/3 cup cold butter

1 egg

2 tablespoons cold water

**FILLING:**

2 tablespoons butter

1 large yellow onion, coarsely chopped

1 tablespoon water

2 teaspoons sugar

1/4 cup Shafer Vineyards Port

1 cup milk

2 whole eggs

2 egg yolks

Freshly ground pepper to taste

1/2 cup walnuts, finely chopped

1 cup crumbled Gorgonzola cheese

*(recipe continued on next page)*

❧ Preheat oven to 350° F.

**For the pastry:** In a large bowl, blend flour and butter with a pastry blender until mixture resembles coarse meal. In a small bowl, stir together the egg and 2 tablespoons water. Pour over flour mixture and stir until just combined and dough forms a ball. Gently flatten dough into a disk and chill for 15 minutes. Roll out dough on a lightly floured surface and fit into a 10-inch quiche dish or pie plate. Prick pastry all over with a fork. Chill until ready to fill.

**For the filling:** In a large skillet, melt butter over medium-low heat. Add the onions, 1 tablespoon water, and sugar and stir to coat the onions with butter. Cover and cook, stirring occasionally, until onions are a dark golden color, about 20 to 30 minutes. Pour in port and stir to blend well. Simmer for about 5 minutes or until liquid has almost evaporated. Remove from heat.

In a bowl, whisk together the milk, eggs, egg yolks, and pepper until smooth. Set aside.

Remove pastry from refrigerator and sprinkle walnuts over the bottom. Spread caramelized onions over the walnuts. Sprinkle the crumbled

*From wine what*
*sudden friendship springs!*

**John Gay**

Gorgonzola over the onions. Pour the milk mixture over the cheese. Bake for about 45 minutes, or until custard is set and the top is golden. Serve warm in small wedges.

*Serves 8 to 10*
*Serve with Shafer Vineyards Port*

**DOMAINE CHARBAY**

1995 Napa Valley

**CABERNET SAUVIGNON**

St. Helena, California
Alc. 13.4% by Vol.

## DOMAINE CHARBAY
## WINERY & DISTILLERY

*Domaine Charbay, a truly artisanal distillery and winery, is the home of master distiller and winemaker Miles Karakasevic. With his wife Susan and their two adult children, Marko and Lara, he produces astounding small-production releases of wines, ports, eaux de vie, liqueurs, and exquisite brandies from their traditional alembic still and winery. Located high above St. Helena atop Spring Mountain, the "still on the hill" is often the site of spontaneous gatherings of family and friends. The enjoyment of simple food along with their handmade wine and spirits is part of the convivial hospitality, which has become their trademark.*

# GIBANICA

*This savory Yugoslavian cheese pastry is delicious served hot, warm, or cold.*

2 1/2 cups cottage cheese

1 1/4 cups sour cream

1 1/4 cups plain yogurt

2/3 cup cream cheese

2/3 cup crumbled feta cheese

1/3 cup heavy cream

3 eggs

1 teaspoon salt

1/2 teaspoon freshly ground black pepper

8 ounces phyllo dough, thawed

3/4 cup melted butter

Preheat oven to 400° F. Generously butter a 13 x 9-inch baking pan.

In a large bowl, blend the cottage cheese, sour cream, yogurt, cream cheese, feta cheese, cream, eggs, salt, and pepper until smooth.

Unfold the phyllo sheets. Use only one sheet at a time and keep the remaining sheets covered with a damp tea towel to keep them from drying out.

*(recipe continued on next page)*

Place one sheet of phyllo in the bottom of the pan. Using a pastry brush, lightly brush the phyllo with butter. Lay a second sheet on top of the first and brush with butter. Spread $1^1/2$ cups of filling evenly over the phyllo. Lay a sheet of phyllo on top of the filling and brush with butter. Lay a second sheet on top and brush with butter. Spread $1^1/2$ cups filling over phyllo. Continue layering with 2 sheets phyllo and $1^1/2$ cups filling until all is used, ending with 2 sheets phyllo. Brush top with remaining melted butter. With a sharp knife, randomly poke 12 holes in the gibanica.

Bake for 30 minutes. Reduce oven to 350° F and bake an additional 45 minutes, or until golden brown. Remove from oven and cool 10 minutes before cutting into squares.

*Serves 24*
*Serve with Domaine Charbay*
*Cabernet Sauvignon*

## IRON HORSE VINEYARDS

*Ten miles from the Pacific coast and sixty-five miles north of San Francisco lies Iron Horse Vineyards, named for the railroad stop it once was. Barry and Audrey Sterling, along with their partner and vineyard manager Forrest Tancer, have developed Iron Horse into one of the premier wineries in the United States. In addition to their well-known and sought-after sparkling wines, they produce outstanding still wines from their vineyards in Sonoma County's Green and Alexander Valleys. The Sterlings and Forrest all live on their land and give daily care and attention to their vineyards, thus assuring consistency and high quality wines.*

# CORN PANCAKES
## *with Caviar*
## *& Crème Fraîche*

*These little pancakes are so sensational,
it would be easy to make a full meal
of them.*

1 cup all-purpose flour

2/3 cup cornmeal

1/2 teaspoon salt

1/2 teaspoon sugar

2 eggs

1 tablespoon melted butter

1 cup milk

3/4 cup corn kernels

3 tablespoons olive oil

1 cup crème fraîche or sour cream

2 ounces black lumpfish caviar

In a large bowl, stir together flour, cornmeal, salt, and sugar. In a small bowl, whisk together eggs and melted butter until smooth. Whisk milk into egg mixture until smooth. Pour milk mixture into flour mixture and whisk until smooth. Stir in corn.

In a large skillet, heat olive oil over medium-high heat. Ladle about 2 tablespoons of batter for each pancake into the hot skillet. Cook until golden brown on both sides. Put a dollop of crème fraîche on each corn pancake and top with a spoonful of caviar. Serve warm.

*Makes about 24*
*Serve with Iron Horse Vineyards*
*Blanc de Blancs*

*Drink no longer water,*
*but use a little wine for thy*
*stomach's sake.*

**The Bible**

## HESS COLLECTION WINERY

*The Hess Collection embraces both art and wine passionately. Their commitment to quality is evident in the contemporary paintings and sculpture lining the galleries of the Visitor Center. It is also evident inside each bottle of their wine—from the acclaimed Hess Collection label to the popular Hess Select wines. Born of a desire to offer distinctive products at reasonable prices, The Hess Collection has embarked on a global journey. The Hess Collection New World Wines has formed partnerships with family-owned producers from Chile, South Africa, Argentina, and Italy who share the common thread of commitment to excellence.*

# PAN-SEARED DIVER SCALLOPS *with* *Pancetta, Whipped Potatoes & Chardonnay Butter Sauce*

*Katie Sutton created this incredibly rich first course for a truly decadent meal.*

## CHARDONNAY BUTTER SAUCE:

2 ounces applewood smoked bacon, diced

1/2 cup Hess Collection Chardonnay

2 shallots, chopped

1 bay leaf

1 sprig fresh thyme

1/2 cup heavy cream

1 cup cold butter, cut into small pieces

## PANCETTA WHIPPED POTATOES:

2 ounces pancetta, diced

2 potatoes, peeled and quartered

1/2 cup heavy cream

1/4 cup butter

2 tablespoons finely chopped chives

Salt and freshly ground black pepper

12 diver scallops

Salt

1 tablespoon olive oil

*(recipe continued on next page)*

**For the sauce:** In a saucepan, cook the bacon over medium heat until just barely cooked. Add the wine, shallots, bay leaf, and thyme and simmer until mixture is reduced to a syrupy consistency. Add cream and simmer until mixture is reduced and very thick. Reduce heat to low. Whisk in the cold butter, a little at a time, until all is incorporated and mixture is creamy. Pour through a sieve and discard the solids. Keep the sauce barely warm; do not let it simmer or the sauce will separate.

**For the potatoes:** In a skillet, cook the pancetta over medium heat until crisp. Set aside. In a large pot, cook the potatoes over medium-high heat in plenty of salted water until tender. Drain well. Mash potatoes with the cream and butter until smooth. Stir in the reserved pancetta and chives. Season with salt and pepper and keep warm.

Season the scallops with salt. In a large skillet, heat the olive oil over high heat. When oil starts to smoke, add the scallops in one layer. Sear for about 2 minutes, then turn and sear on the other side until just cooked through. Do not crowd scallops in the skillet or they will stew rather than be seared.

Divide the potatoes onto six plates. Top with 2 scallops and ladle the sauce around the potatoes.

*Serves 6*
*Serve with Hess Collection*
*Chardonnay*

PRODUCED & BOTTLED BY FROG'S LEAP, RUTHERFORD, CA

## FROG'S LEAP WINERY

*A strong commitment to sustainable agriculture along with the winery's goal of having fun explains much of what Frog's Leap stands for. After founding the winery in 1981 on a site known as the Frog Farm, John and Julie Williams rebuilt the century-old winery building into the home of some of the Napa Valley's finest wines. The winery's motto—"Time's fun when you're having flies"— reflects the tongue-in-cheek approach John and Julie take toward producing their excellent wines.*

# GRILLED PRAWNS

*These tasty yet messy grilled prawns are*
*served in the shell, so you'll want to have*
*a stack of napkins and lemon-scented*
*fingerbowls ready for your guests.*

24 large prawns, with shells on

1/2 cup chopped fresh basil

1/4 cup olive oil

1/4 cup Frog's Leap Winery Sauvignon Blanc

3 cloves garlic, minced

1 teaspoon salt

1/2 teaspoon dried red chile flakes

1/4 teaspoon freshly ground black pepper

Place the prawns in a shallow dish just large enough to hold them in one layer. In a bowl, whisk together the basil, olive oil, wine, garlic, salt, chile flakes, and pepper. Pour over the prawns, cover, and chill for 1 hour.

Prepare the grill. Grill the prawns on both sides until the shells turn pink. Serve immediately.

*Serves 6*
*Serve with Frog's Leap Winery*
*Sauvignon Blanc*

## BERINGER VINEYARDS

*The oldest continually operating winery in the Napa Valley was started in 1876 by Jacob and Frederick Beringer, immigrants from Mainz, Germany. Currently a publicly traded company, owned by thousands of wine-loving shareholders, Beringer Vineyards excels in the production of vineyard-designated reds, graceful and supple whites, as well as lovingly tended late harvest dessert wines.*

# CHILLED GRILLED PRAWNS *with Bloody Mary Sauce & Avocado Mousse*

*Jerry Comfort, Beringer Vineyard's executive chef, created the perfect first course for a warm Napa Valley summer evening.*

## BLOODY MARY SAUCE:

1 tablespoon olive oil

2 ribs celery, chopped

1 red bell pepper, chopped

1 small white onion, chopped

1 clove garlic, chopped

10 Roma tomatoes, chopped

2 tablespoons freshly squeezed lime juice

1 tablespoon Worcestershire sauce

1 1/2 teaspoons freshly grated horseradish

1 1/2 teaspoons Tabasco sauce

1/2 teaspoon freshly ground black pepper

## AVOCADO MOUSSE:

2 avocados

1 tablespoon freshly squeezed lime juice

$1/2$ teaspoon salt

1 cup heavy cream

2 tablespoons olive oil

Corn tortillas, thinly sliced into ribbons

18 large prawns, peeled with the tails left on

Olive oil

Sliced limes and celery leaves, for garnish

🍂 **For the sauce:** In a large pot, heat the olive oil over medium-high heat. Add the celery, bell peppers, onion, and garlic and sauté until tender. Add tomatoes, reduce heat to low, and simmer for about 30 minutes, stirring often. Remove from heat and place in a blender. Blend until smooth and strain through a fine sieve into a bowl. Discard solids. Whisk in lime juice, Worcestershire sauce, horseradish, Tabasco sauce, and pepper. Cover and chill.

*(recipe continued on next page)*

**For the mousse:** In the bowl of a food processor, combine avocado, lime juice, and salt and process until smooth. In a large bowl, whip cream to soft peaks. Gently fold in avocado mixture until smooth. Cover and chill.

In a large skillet, heat olive oil over medium-high heat. Add tortilla ribbons and fry until crisp. Drain on paper towels. Set aside.

Prepare the grill. Brush prawns with olive oil and grill until cooked through.

Spoon sauce onto six plates. Place 3 prawns around the plate and put a large dollop of avocado mousse in the center. Top with fried tortillas. Garnish with sliced limes and celery leaves.

*Serves 6*
*Serve with Beringer Vineyards*
*White Meritage*

# GOAT CHEESECAKE
## *with Roasted Pepper Purée*
## *& Herb Oil*

*California wine country cuisine is showcased
perfectly in this savory cheesecake from Beringer
Vineyard's executive chef, Jerry Comfort.*

**HERB OIL:**

1 bunch fresh basil

1 bunch fresh tarragon

1 bunch fresh chervil

1 1/2 cups vegetable oil

**GOAT CHEESECAKE:**

1 pound cream cheese

10 ounces goat cheese

4 eggs

1 cup heavy cream

**ROASTED PEPPER PURÉE:**

2 yellow bell peppers, cut in half and seeded

2 red bell peppers, cut in half and seeded

1/4 cup olive oil

4 teaspoons freshly squeezed lemon juice, divided

🌿 **For the herb oil:** Trim off the leaves from the herbs and discard the stems. Blanch the herbs in boiling salted water for 10 seconds, drain, then plunge into a bowl of ice water. Drain well. Purée in a blender then transfer to a bowl. Gently stir in the oil. Let the mixture infuse overnight, stirring occasionally. The next day, ladle off the brilliant green oil and discard the solids. Pour into a clean jar and cover. Store in the refrigerator.

**For the goat cheesecake:** Preheat the oven to 350° F. Lightly oil a 9-inch springform pan and line with parchment. Lightly oil the parchment.

In a large bowl, beat the cream cheese and the goat cheese together until well blended. Add the eggs, one at a time, beating well after each addition. Stir in the cream until smooth. Pour batter into prepared pan and place in a larger pan filled with enough water to come halfway up the sides of the springform pan. Bake for about 45 to 55 minutes, or until the top is almost set but still a little loose in the center. Cool, then cover and chill for at least 4 hours or overnight.

**For the roasted pepper purée:** Preheat oven to 450° F. Lightly oil a baking sheet.

Brush the bell peppers with the olive oil and place on the prepared baking sheet. Roast the peppers for about 30 minutes or until blackened. Remove from oven and place hot peppers in a plastic bag. Let them steam in the bag until cool. Remove the skins and discard. Place the yellow bell peppers in a blender with 2 teaspoons of the lemon juice and purée until smooth. Pour into a small bowl. Place the red bell peppers in a blender with the remaining 2 teaspoons of lemon juice and purée. Place in a separate bowl.

**To assemble:** Drizzle plates with 1 tablespoon each of the red and yellow bell pepper purées. Pour on 1 tablespoon of the herb oil. Place a thin slice of goat cheesecake in the center.

*Serves 8 to 10*
*Serve with Beringer Knights Valley*
*White Meritage*

# FETA CHEESE & SUNDRIED TOMATO STRUDEL

*The crisp flaky slices of hot strudel are a delightful counterpoint to the delicate texture of baby greens in this wonderful salad from Jerry Comfort.*

8 ounces feta cheese, crumbled

$1/2$ cup sundried tomatoes in oil, drained and minced

$1/4$ cup chopped kalamata olives

2 tablespoons chopped fresh basil

2 tablespoons pine nuts, lightly toasted

1 teaspoon freshly ground black pepper

8 ounces filo dough, thawed

$1/2$ cup olive oil

## SALAD:

1 cup Beringer Vineyards Knights Valley Cabernet Sauvignon

$1/2$ cup olive oil

1 pound baby salad greens

❧ Preheat oven to 425° F. Lightly oil a baking sheet.

In a bowl, combine feta, sundried tomatoes, olives, basil, pine nuts, and pepper and toss until well combined.

Unfold the filo sheets. Use only one sheet at a time and keep the remaining sheets covered with a damp tea towel to keep them from drying out. Lay one sheet on a cutting board. Using a pastry brush, brush the filo with olive oil. Lay a second sheet on top of the first and brush with olive oil. Continue layering and brushing with olive oil until you have used 4 sheets of filo.

Place half of the feta mixture in a row at the bottom of the filo. Roll up tightly and slice $1^1\!/2$-inches thick. Place cut side up on baking sheet. Bake for 8 to 10 minutes, or until golden brown. Repeat with remaining filo and feta mixture.

**For the salad:** In a small saucepan, reduce Knights Valley Cabernet Sauvignon over medium heat to 2 tablespoons. Cool. Whisk in olive oil. Toss with salad greens and divide onto 4 plates. Top with hot strudel slices.

*Serves 4*
*Serve with Beringer Vineyards Knights Valley*
*Cabernet Sauvignon*

## BELVEDERE VINEYARDS AND WINERY

*In Italian, Belvedere means "beautiful view," which aptly describes the vista from this rustic redwood winery in the Russian River Valley. The winery was built in 1982, the same year owners Bill and Sally Hambrecht bought their first piece of vineyard land high atop Bradford Mountain in Dry Creek Valley. Over the years they purchased and planted additional estate vineyards in the Dry Creek, Alexander, and Russian River Valleys in northern Sonoma County. As Bill Hambrecht often says, "Our most valuable asset is our vineyards. Good vineyards are as valuable as gold to a winery, and Belvedere has access to some of Sonoma County's best."*

# SIZZLING SHRIMP
## *in Garlic Sauce*

*Chef Antonio Buenvia of San Francisco's Vinga Restaurant has recreated this stunning but simple tapas dish from his native Catalan region of Spain.*

24 large shrimp, peeled and deveined

1/4 cup olive oil

4 cloves garlic, thinly sliced

2 serrano chiles, seeded and thinly sliced

1 teaspoon coarse salt

In a large skillet, heat olive oil over medium-high heat. When oil is almost smoking, add shrimp. Sauté until just barely pink on both sides. Add garlic and chiles and sauté until fragrant. Sprinkle with salt. Serve sizzling.

*Serves 4 to 6*
*Serve with Belvedere Vineyards*
*and Winery Chardonnay*

## VIANSA WINERY

*On the evening of January 29, 1988, on a hill near Sonoma, Sam and Vicki Sebastiani opened a bottle of sparkling wine and toasted the land that would one day see their dream a reality. Their winery, Viansa, would embody a proud Italian heritage, and it would over-look a lowland shared by vineyards and nearly 100 acres of restored natural wetlands. Today, Viansa is a reality welcoming visitors from around the world, and they invite you to share your wedding, special event, or meeting with them. The wines and food of Viansa are among the world's finest, and the wetlands provide critical habitat to countless water-fowl, animals, and aquatic life.*

# CALAMARI CON SALSA DI CAPPERI
## *(Calamari with Caper Sauce)*

*Everyone loves fried calamari. This lower-fat version, from Cucina Viansa by Vicki Sebastiani, is sprinkled with the minimal amount of olive oil and baked, instead of being deep-fried.*

**CAPER SAUCE:**

1 cup mayonnaise

1/4 cup capers, minced

1/4 cup freshly squeezed lemon juice

2 teaspoons minced fresh thyme

2 cloves garlic, minced


3 pounds calamari (squid) bodies and tentacles, cleaned

2 cups dry unseasoned breadcrumbs

2 tablespoons minced fresh thyme

2 teaspoons salt

1/2 teaspoon freshly ground black pepper

1/3 cup Viansa Extra Virgin Olive Oil

*(recipe continued on next page)*

**For the sauce:** In a bowl, stir together all ingredients until well mixed. Cover and chill 30 minutes to allow flavors to blend.

**For the calamari:** Preheat oven to 450° F. Lightly oil a jelly roll pan.

Rinse calamari and cut the bodies into 1/2-inch rings. Pat dry thoroughly with paper towels. This is crucial so that the breading does not become soggy. Set aside.

In a large bowl, stir together breadcrumbs, thyme, salt, and pepper. Add the calamari and toss to coat evenly. Place calamari on prepared pan and drizzle olive oil over the top. With 2 spatulas, toss gently to distribute the oil evenly. Bake for 10 minutes. Toss gently, then bake an additional 10 minutes, or until golden brown. Serve immediately with the caper sauce.

*Serves 8*
*Serve with Viansa Winery*
*Chardonnay*

## TREFETHEN VINEYARDS

*Tradition combines with technology at Trefethen Vineyards, where a century-old winery and the latest in winemaking equipment give the Trefethen family, and their wines, the best of both worlds. First planted with grapes in the 1850s, the Eshcol ranch, as it was known back then, received its name from a biblical allusion to an immense cluster of grapes. In 1968, Gene and Katie Trefethen revitalized the old Eshcol property and planted new vines on the 600-acre valley estate and on fifty acres to the northwest. The first wines were vinified in 1973, and today wine production has climbed to 75,000 cases per year. The Trefethen family has this to say about their wines: "Winemaking is part agriculture and part parenting. We are proud to introduce you to what we have worried over and cared for—our wines. They are meant to be shared and enjoyed among friends."*

# MUSSELS
## *in Thyme Beurre Blanc*

*This sophisticated, elegant first course is
actually quick and simple to prepare. So
enjoy it with a group of your best friends.*

1 cup Trefethen Vineyards Chardonnay

2 tablespoons white wine vinegar

2 shallots, minced

1 teaspoon thyme

$1/2$ teaspoon salt

3 tablespoons heavy cream

$1/2$ cup cold butter, cut into small pieces

1 tablespoon minced fresh chives

48 mussels, scrubbed and debearded

3 cups water

In a saucepan, whisk together wine, vinegar,
shallots, thyme, and salt. Bring to a simmer over
medium heat and simmer until mixture is reduced
to $1/4$ cup. Whisk in cream and bring to a simmer.
Remove saucepan from heat. Whisk in butter, one
piece at a time, until all butter is incorporated. Stir
in chives and keep barely warm. Do not let simmer
or sauce will separate.

In a large pot, combine mussels and water. Cover pot and bring to a boil over high heat. Steam for about 3 minutes until mussels open. Discard any mussels that do not open. With a slotted spoon, remove mussels and divide into six bowls. Spoon a little sauce into the mussels and serve immediately.

*Serves 6*
*Serve with Trefethen Vineyards*
*Chardonnay*

*It is better to hide ignorance,*
*but it is hard to do*
*when we relax over wine.*

**Heraclitus**

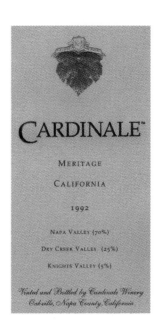

## CARDINALE

*Cardinale Rule: Make grape selection an obsession and gentle winemaking a virtue. Grow fruit of intense vineyard and varietal character from the finest sites in the Mayacamas. Pick only when the fruit is physiologically ripe and balanced in flavor. Hand harvest into small lug boxes, during the cool of the morning. Keep each vineyard separate, in order to know it better. Hand sort all fruit and use only sound, ripe berries. Carefully crack the berries and begin native yeast fermentation. Let juice and skins macerate gently for twenty-five to thirty-five days to maximize flavor and texture. Use a traditional basket press to deepen mid-palate flavors. Place into 100 percent new tight-grained French oak château barrels. Attentively rack wine from barrel to barrel every three months. Age in barrel for eighteen to twenty-one months. Bottle unfiltered. Age in bottle for twelve months before release. Enjoy or bottle age for an additional five to ten years.*

# SMOKED SALMON CAKES

*To make ahead of time, place uncooked salmon cakes between sheets of waxed paper and freeze.*

8 ounces smoked salmon, flaked

1/2 cup fine dry breadcrumbs

1/4 cup minced celery

1/4 cup minced onion

1/4 cup minced parsley

2 tablespoons minced chives

1/2 teaspoon freshly ground black pepper

2 eggs, lightly beaten

Additional breadcrumbs for coating

3 tablespoons vegetable oil

In a large bowl, combine smoked salmon, 1/2 cup breadcrumbs, celery, onion, parsley, chives, and pepper and mix well. Add the eggs and stir until mixture is evenly moistened. Place breadcrumbs in a shallow bowl. Roll salmon mixture into walnut-sized balls and coat with breadcrumbs. Flatten slightly and place on a baking sheet. Cover and chill for 1 hour.

*(recipe continued on next page)*

In a large nonstick skillet, heat oil over medium-high heat. Carefully place the salmon cakes in the hot oil and cook until golden brown on both sides. Serve hot.

*Makes about 24 cakes*
*Serve with Cardinale Royale*

*Wine that maketh glad*
*the heart of man.*
**The Bible**

## HUSCH VINEYARDS

*Husch Vineyards is a small family winery and the first bonded winery located in the Anderson Valley appellation of Mendocino County in northern California, a picturesque two-and-a-half hour drive north of San Francisco. All Husch wines are made from grapes grown in the family-owned vineyards. Some of the wines are distributed throughout the United States, but many are available only locally or at their tasting room. Quality is the key word at the winery. It shows in the care that goes into growing fine grapes, in the attention given in each step of the winemaking process, and in the time given to visitors who come to the winery for tastings.*

*sweet* 8/7/06

# SPICY ORANGE DRUMETTES

*Tangy and flavorful, but easy and fun to make, these are perennial picnic and party favorites. No matter how many napkins you supply, your guests will be licking their fingers and begging for more!*

3 tablespoons olive oil

36 chicken drumettes

1 cup sugar

$1/4$ cup water

$1/2$ cup balsamic vinegar

Juice of 2 oranges

$1/2$ cup black bean sauce

Zest of 2 oranges, finely minced

2 teaspoons minced fresh ginger

In a large skillet, heat the oil over medium heat. Add the chicken and sauté until well browned on all sides and cooked through.

In a heavy saucepan, bring the sugar and water to a boil over medium-high heat, swirling the pan often to blend. Cook until the sugar caramelizes and turns golden brown. Whisk in the vinegar and orange juice, taking care since it may splatter up. Whisk until smooth, then add the black bean sauce, zest, and ginger. Pour over chicken and stir until well coated.

*Serves 6*
*Serve with Husch Vineyards*
*Gewürztraminer*

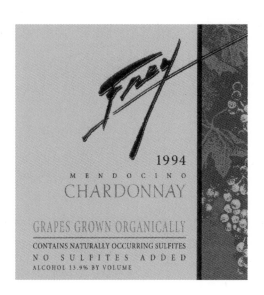

## FREY VINEYARDS

*A member of California Certified Organic Farmers, Frey Vineyards was one of the first to farm their vineyards organically and offer a wine from certified organically grown grapes. Located near the northernmost origins of the Russian River watershed, this Mendocino-appellation winery produces elegant, well-structured wines from its dry-farmed vineyards.*

# AVOCADO AND PINK GRAPEFRUIT SALAD
## *with Butter Lettuce &*
## *Gewürztraminer-Raspberry Vinaigrette*

*When the weather turns hot, turn to this
crisp and tangy salad to cool down.
Serve with cheese and crusty bread for
a no-fuss country lunch.*

### GEWÜRZTRAMINER RASPBERRY VINAIGRETTE:

1/2 cup olive oil

1/4 cup Frey Vineyards Gewürztraminer

1/4 cup raspberry vinegar

1 tablespoon soy sauce

1 teaspoon finely minced lemon thyme

Freshly ground black pepper


2 pink grapefruit

3 heads butter lettuce, torn into bite-sized
    pieces

1 head radicchio, thinly sliced

2 avocados, peeled and cut into 8 wedges

1 torpedo red onion, sliced into thin rings

*(recipe continued on next page)*

🍇 **For the vinaigrette:** In a bowl, whisk together olive oil, wine, vinegar, soy sauce, lemon thyme, and black pepper.

With a small sharp knife, trim the peel and pith from grapefruit. Cut out the sections, following along the membranes.

On six chilled plates, divide butter lettuce. Top with sliced radicchio. Arrange grapefruit sections and avocado wedges in an alternating spiral on top. Scatter red onion rings over the top. Sprinkle vinaigrette over salads and serve immediately.

*Serves 6*
*Serve with Frey Vineyards*
*Gewürztraminer*

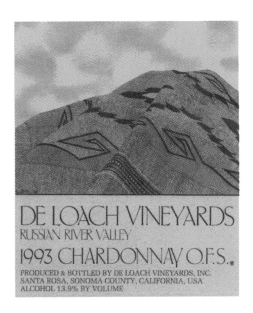

## DE LOACH
## VINEYARDS

*The morning fog along the Russian River Valley, a product of marine influence, is instrumental for the quality of Cecil and Christine De Loach's estate-grown wines. This cooling influence in the heat of late summer allows their vines to fully develop their fruit while maintaining acidity and elegance. Cecil and Christine De Loach's personal connection to their vineyards and cellar ensures a consistency of style and excellence in quality year after year.*

# SALAD OF BABY GREENS *with Toasted Pine Nut Vinaigrette*

*This is a simple yet sublimely seasoned salad.*

$2/3$ cup pine nuts

$1/2$ cup olive oil

3 tablespoons white wine vinegar

$1/2$ teaspoon salt

$1/2$ teaspoon tarragon

$1/8$ teaspoon freshly grated nutmeg

$3/4$ teaspoon finely minced lemon zest

White pepper

$1 1/2$ pounds mixed baby greens

Preheat oven to 350° F.

Spread pine nuts on a baking sheet. Bake for about 5 minutes, or until pine nuts are lightly toasted. Let cool.

In a bowl, whisk together olive oil, vinegar, salt, tarragon, and nutmeg. Whisk in lemon zest and white pepper. Toss dressing with baby greens and divide onto six plates. Spoon pine nuts on top.

*Serves 6*
*Serve with De Loach Vineyards*
*Russian River Valley Chardonnay*

## DOMAINE CARNEROS

*Designed after Château de la Marquetterie in Champagne, with its roots in the French house of Taittinger, Domaine Carneros is the only sparkling wine producer using exclusively Carneros grapes for their super-premium méthode-champenoise. Situated atop a knoll surrounded by its vineyards, the château commands a spectacular view of the rolling hills of Carneros. Pinot Noir and Chardonnay, along with a lesser amount of Pinot Meunier, serve as the basis of Domaine Carneros' elegant and delicate sparkling wines.*

# BABY GREENS *with* *Goat Cheese, Dried Figs &* *Sesame Vinaigrette*

*The sweet and chewy figs in this summer salad are a delightful counterpoint to the tangy goat cheese.*

### SESAME VINAIGRETTE:

1/4 cup olive oil

3 tablespoons sesame seeds

2 tablespoons sesame oil

2 tablespoons balsamic vinegar

1 tablespoon Domaine Carneros
    Sparkling Wine

1 tablespoon tahini

1 tablespoon minced shallots

1 clove garlic, minced

1/2 teaspoon salt

1/4 teaspoon freshly ground black pepper

1/4 teaspoon lime juice


1 pound mixed baby greens

8 ounces dried Mission figs, quartered

6 ounces goat cheese, crumbled

**For the sesame vinaigrette:** In a blender, combine all ingredients and blend until smooth.

In a large bowl, combine greens, figs, and goat cheese. Pour sesame vinaigrette over and toss gently.

*Serves 4*
*Serve with Domaine Carneros*
*Sparkling Wine*

*Bring water, bring wine, boy!*
*Bring flower garlands to me!*
*Yes, bring them, so that I may*
*try a bout with love.*

**Anacreon**

## ALDERBROOK VINEYARDS AND WINERY

*The Dry Creek Valley, just to the west of Healdsburg, is home to Alderbrook Vineyards and Winery. Purchased by George Gillemot in 1991, Alderbrook has been on an upward course ever since. Chardonnay, Sauvignon Blanc, Gewürztraminer, Zinfandel, Pinot Noir, Syrah, Merlot, Cabernet Sauvignon, and Viognier are among the wines produced by this medal-winning winery. The quality of Alderbrook's wines can be directly traced to their stated goal: "To produce the very finest wines of the Dry Creek Valley."*

# SUNDRIED PEAR & GOAT CHEESE SALAD

*Winery chef Jim May came up with this quintessential California pairing of tangy goat cheese, dried pears, and an aromatic vinaigrette as a counterpoint to a hearty autumn or winter meal.*

4 dried pear halves, diced

2 tablespoons Alderbrook Winery
 Sauvignon Blanc

4 ounces marinated goat cheese

4 strips bacon, diced

2 cloves garlic, minced

$1/2$ cup Alderbrook Winery Sauvignon Blanc

1 tablespoon balsamic vinegar

1 tablespoon freshly squeezed lemon juice

2 teaspoons minced fresh thyme

1 teaspoon minced lemon zest

1 teaspoon Dijon mustard

4 cups mixed salad greens

*(recipe continued on next page)*

🍃 In a small bowl, combine pears and 2 tablespoons of the wine. Cover and let sit overnight.

Drain marinated goat cheese and reserve 1/4 cup of the marinade. Crumble the cheese. If you cannot find marinated goat cheese, use regular goat cheese and 1/4 cup olive oil.

In a skillet, cook bacon over medium heat until almost crisp. Pour off excess fat, add garlic, and sauté until fragrant. Whisk in reserved marinade, pears and their liquid, 1/2 cup wine, vinegar, lemon juice, thyme, lemon zest, and mustard and reduce heat to low. Stir in half of the goat cheese and whisk until smooth. Place greens in a large bowl. Pour warm dressing over and toss to coat. Sprinkle remaining goat cheese on top and serve immediately.

*Serves 4*
*Serve with Alderbrook Winery*
*Sauvignon Blanc*

FLORA SPRINGS
1994 SANGIOVESE
NAPA VALLEY

ALC. 13.0% BY VOL.

## FLORA SPRINGS

*Flora Springs is a family endeavor that epitomizes hard work, dedication, and teamwork. The vitality of the family is obvious as they set about the task of growing great grapes and making delicious wine. Even the name Flora Springs has significance—Flora is the name of the family matriarch, and the springs refer to the water source on the property that has flowed uninterrupted regardless of periods of drought.*

# TOMATO & BUFFALO MOZZARELLA SALAD
## *with Caramelized Onions & Lemon Vinaigrette*

*The Chaminade Restaurant at Santa Cruz came up with this fresh and exciting salad. Make up the caramelized onions in advance for a quick-to-finish first course.*

### LEMON VINAIGRETTE:

1 tablespoon butter

2 shallots, minced

1/2 cup white wine vinegar

1/4 cup freshly squeezed lemon juice

2 tablespoons sugar

1/2 teaspoon salt

1/4 teaspoon white pepper

1 cup olive oil

1 cup lightly packed basil leaves, minced

### CARAMELIZED ONIONS:

2 tablespoons olive oil

2 red onions, chopped

1 tablespoon water

1 teaspoon sugar

4 cups arugula, torn into bite-sized pieces

3 cups baby spinach, torn into bite-sized pieces

1 head raddichio, finely sliced

6 Roma tomatoes, sliced

6 ounces fresh buffalo mozzarella, sliced

**For the vinaigrette:** In a saucepan, melt butter over medium heat. Add shallots and sauté until translucent. Whisk in vinegar, lemon juice, sugar, salt, and white pepper and bring to a boil. Reduce heat to medium-low and simmer for 3 minutes. Remove from heat, let cool slightly, and whisk in olive oil. Let cool completely, then stir in basil. Set aside.

**For the onions:** In a nonstick skillet, heat olive oil over medium heat. Add onions and sauté until tender. Stir in water and sugar, reduce heat to low, and cover tightly. Cook, stirring occasionally, until very thick and dark, about 30 minutes.

In a large bowl, combine arugula, spinach, and raddichio. Pour in dressing and toss gently to coat. Divide greens onto six plates. Divide tomatoes and mozzarella on top of greens. Top with a spoonful of caramelized onions.

*Serves 6*
*Serve with Flora Springs*
*Sangiovese*

# ROBERT MONDAVI
# WINERY

*Founded in 1966 by Robert Mondavi and his son, Michael, the Robert Mondavi Winery is considered a leader in the modern wine industry. They are committed to producing naturally balanced wines of great finesse and elegance that complement and enhance fine food. They have been successful in achieving these goals through earth-friendly farming practices, a sophisticated winery emphasizing gentle treatment of their wines, and a genuine love for their handiwork. No other winery epitomizes the Napa Valley like the Robert Mondavi Winery.*

# SALAD OF ROMAINE HEARTS *with Goat Cheese & Fumé Blanc Vinaigrette*

*Tangy goat cheese is one of my personal favorite salad ingredients. This combination from Sarah Scott, the executive chef at Robert Mondavi Winery, is simply excellent.*

## FUMÉ BLANC VINAIGRETTE:

1 1/2 cups Robert Mondavi Winery Fumé Blanc

2 shallots, minced

1/2 teaspoon finely minced lemon zest

1 tablespoon freshly squeezed lemon juice

1 1/2 teaspoons rice vinegar

Salt and freshly ground black pepper

3/4 cup olive oil


## GARLIC CROUTONS:

1/4 cup melted butter

4 cloves garlic, minced

Salt and freshly ground black pepper

1 baguette, cut into 1-inch cubes


3 hearts of romaine lettuce

4 ounces fresh goat cheese, crumbled

Chopped Italian parsley for garnish

*(recipe continued on next page)*

**For the vinaigrette:** In a small saucepan, simmer wine over medium heat until reduced to $1/2$ cup. Remove from heat and stir in shallots and lemon zest. Let cool to room temperature. When cooled, whisk in lemon juice, vinegar, salt, and pepper. Whisk in olive oil and set aside.

**For the croutons:** Preheat oven to 350° F. Lightly oil a baking sheet. Stir together melted butter, garlic, salt, and pepper. Place the bread cubes on prepared baking sheet and drizzle the butter mixture over the top. Toss to coat evenly. Bake for about 10 minutes, or until lightly toasted.

In a large bowl, toss together the lettuce and goat cheese. Pour the vinaigrette over and toss to coat evenly. Divide onto six plates and top with croutons and parsley.

*Serves 6*
*Serve with Robert Mondavi Winery*
*Fumé Blanc*

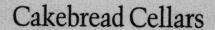

# Cakebread Cellars

NAPA VALLEY
## Sauvignon Blanc
### 1997

ALCOHOL 13.5% BY VOLUME

## CAKEBREAD CELLARS

*A true family winery, Cakebread Cellars in Rutherford is one of the most creative and successful wineries in California's famed Napa Valley. Since its founding in 1973, the winery has developed a reputation for producing world-class wines and pairing them with outstanding cuisine. Dolores Cakebread, the winery's culinary director, had the vision to plant vegetable gardens at the same time their vineyards were being planted. She has been a forerunner in the development of California cuisine, which emphasizes fresh, natural, and locally grown produce to complement the wines of Cakebread Cellars.*

# ROASTED BEET
# & SPINACH SALAD
## *with Candied Pecans*
## *& Goat Cheese*

*This salad is very colorful when made with
a mixture of red, gold, and chioggia beets.*

**CANDIED PECANS:**

1 tablespoon honey

1 tablespoon sugar

1 tablespoon water

1/8 teaspoon salt

1 cup pecans

**SHERRY VINAIGRETTE:**

1/4 cup sherry vinegar

1 shallot, minced

1 cup olive oil

Salt and freshly ground black pepper

3 bunches baby beets, tops and tails removed

1 tablespoon chopped fresh dill

4 ounces baby spinach

3 ounces goat cheese, crumbled

**For the pecans:** Preheat oven to 350° F. Lightly
oil 2 baking sheets. In a small saucepan, combine
honey, sugar, water, and salt. Bring to a boil over
high heat until sugar dissolves. Stir in pecans and

continue cooking until the pecans are completely covered with the syrup and the bottom of the pan is almost dry. Pour pecans onto one of the prepared baking sheets and spread them into one layer. Bake for about 5 minutes, then stir the nuts. Bake an additional 5 minutes, or until dark golden brown but not burned. Remove from oven and pour the pecans onto the other baking sheet. Refrigerate until cold. Set aside $1/2$ cup of candied pecans for the salad.

**For the vinaigrette:** In a bowl, combine vinegar and shallot. Whisk in olive oil. Season with salt and pepper. Set aside.

Preheat oven to 400° F. Scrub beets well and wrap in foil. Roast beets for about 1 hour, or until very tender. When cool enough to handle, peel and cut into $1/4$-inch slices. Place in a bowl and pour half of the vinaigrette over. Stir in the dill.

In a separate bowl, toss the spinach with the remaining vinaigrette. Divide spinach onto six plates. Top with sliced beets. Sprinkle the goat cheese over the salad and top with the candied pecans.

*Serves 6*
*Serve with Cakebread Cellars*
*Sauvignon Blanc*

## V. SATTUI WINERY

*V. Sattui Winery is a family-owned winery established in 1885 and located in St. Helena, the very heart of California's famous Napa Valley. Their award-winning wines are sold exclusively at the winery, by mail order, and from their website direct to customers. Surrounding the beautiful stone winery is a large tree-shaded picnic ground. V. Sattui also boasts a large gourmet cheese shop and deli.*

# THAI CHICKEN SALAD

*V. Sattui Winery's Robert O'Malley designed this wine-friendly dish. Served by itself, this would make a great luncheon salad.*

## THAI DRESSING:

$1/4$ cup packed brown sugar

$1/4$ cup fish sauce

$1/4$ cup minced fresh basil

$1/4$ cup minced fresh mint

2 serrano chiles, seeded and minced

2 tablespoons soy sauce

1 tablespoon sesame oil

1 tablespoon minced fresh ginger

$1/4$ teaspoon freshly grated nutmeg

4 cups cooked cubed chicken

1 cup bean sprouts

1 stalk celery, chopped

$1/2$ English cucumber, peeled and cut into matchsticks

$1/2$ yellow bell pepper, cut into matchsticks

$1/4$ cup dry-roasted peanuts, chopped

6 mint sprigs for garnish

*(recipe continued on next page)*

🍃 **For the dressing:** In a bowl, combine all ingredients and whisk until sugar dissolves. Set aside.

In a large bowl, combine chicken, bean sprouts, celery, cucumber, and bell pepper. Pour dressing over and toss well. Divide onto six plates. Sprinkle with peanuts and garnish with mint sprigs.

*Serves 6*
*Serve with V. Sattui Winery*
*Chardonnay*

*Let me die in a tavern*
*so that the wine may be near*
*my dying mouth.*

**The Archpoet**

**1995**

**SAUVIGNON BLANC**

LIVERMORE VALLEY, CALIFORNIA

ALC. 12.5% BY VOL

## WENTE BROTHERS
## WINERY

*In the late nineteenth century, Carl Heinrich Wente purchased fifty acres in the Livermore Valley, planted vineyards, and began building a winery. First to varietally label Chardonnay, Sauvignon Blanc, and Sémillon, they quickly gained renown by winning awards at both the Paris Exhibition of 1937 and the World's Fair in San Francisco in 1939. The Wentes have long believed in the importance of the pairing of food and wine. In 1981, they realized a long-term dream and opened their restaurant at the Wente Sparkling Cellars. The restaurant serves up not only their magnificent wines, but also estate-bottled olive oils and homegrown beef off their working ranch.*

# EGGPLANT &
# PEPPER SOUP
## *with Chipotle Cream*

*Wente's executive chef Kimball Jones has
introduced the flavors of old Mexico into a
searingly hot and delicious soup, which
pairs intriguingly with their Grey Riesling.*

1 large eggplant
1 red bell pepper, cut in half
1 small red onion, cut in half
4 cloves garlic
3 tablespoons olive oil
4 cups chicken stock
1 tablespoon balsamic vinegar
1 tablespoon minced parsley
1 bay leaf
1/2 teaspoon minced fresh thyme
Salt and freshly ground black pepper

**CHIPOTLE CREAM:**
1 cup sour cream
1 1/2 teaspoons minced chipotle chile
1/2 teaspoon freshly squeezed lime juice
Salt and freshly ground black pepper

Preheat oven to 350° F. Lightly oil a baking
sheet. Place whole eggplant, bell pepper, onion,

and garlic on prepared baking sheet. Drizzle with olive oil. Bake for about 30 minutes, or until pepper is blackened and eggplant is very soft. Remove from oven and immediately place pepper in a bowl and cover with plastic wrap. When cool enough to handle, peel pepper and set aside. When eggplant is cool enough to handle, cut off stem end. Slice into quarters lengthwise. Place skin-side-down on a cutting board. With the back of a knife, scrape the flesh off the peel. Discard the peel. Set aside.

In a large pot, combine roasted pepper, eggplant flesh, onion, and garlic. Pour in chicken stock, vinegar, parsley, bay leaf, and thyme. Bring to a boil, then reduce heat to low, cover, and simmer 30 minutes. Purée in batches, then return to the pot and keep warm. Season with salt and pepper.

**For the chipotle cream:** In a small bowl, whisk together sour cream, chipotle chile, and lime juice. Season with salt and pepper.

To serve, ladle soup into four bowls and swirl about 3 tablespoons of the chipotle cream into the soup.

*Serves 4 to 6*
*Serve with Wente Estate Winery*
*Grey Riesling*

TOPOLOS
*at Russian River Vineyards*

DRY FARMED

Sonoma Mountain
*Chardonnay*
1994

HILLSIDE

PRODUCED & BOTTLED BY TOPOLOS
AT RUSSIAN RIVER VINEYARDS, FORESTVILLE, CA, USA
WITH ORGANICALLY GROWN GRAPES
ALCOHOL 13% BY VOLUME, CONTAINS SULFITES

## TOPOLOS RUSSIAN RIVER VINEYARDS

*Topolos Russian River Vineyards is a family-owned winery and restaurant in Sonoma County just an hour north of San Francisco and fifteen minutes west of Santa Rosa. Whether you choose to dine outside around the fountain patio or inside by the fireplace, Russian River Vineyards is the ultimate Sonoma County winery experience. The ambience is casual but elegant, and the menus combine authentic Greek cuisine from the Topolos family's recipes with offerings from the rest of the Mediterranean and the chef's creative inventions.*

# CURRIED BROCCOLI SOUP

*This is a great first course from*
*Bob Engle for a winter meal.*

1 tablespoon butter

1 onion, chopped

2 teaspoons curry powder

4 cups chicken stock

3 cups chopped broccoli

2 green apples, peeled and chopped

1 teaspoon salt

1/2 teaspoon white pepper

1/4 teaspoon freshly grated nutmeg

1/2 cup heavy cream

In a large pot, melt butter over medium heat. Add onion and sauté until tender. Sprinkle curry powder over onion and whisk until it is evenly absorbed. Whisk in chicken stock until smooth. Stir in broccoli, apples, salt, pepper, and nutmeg. Reduce heat to medium-low, cover, and simmer until broccoli is very tender. Purée in batches in a blender. Return soup to pot and stir in the cream. Heat through but do not let boil.

*Serves 6*
*Serve with Topolos Russian River Vineyards*
*Chardonnay*

## RODNEY STRONG
## VINEYARDS

*Over thirty-five years ago, Rodney Strong was one of the first to recognize Sonoma County's potential for excellence. After searching for vineyard land that would bring each grape variety to its fullest potential, Rodney Strong finally selected vineyard sites in the Chalk Hill, Alexander Valley, and Russian River Valley appellations to produce his wine. In the cellar, he employs the subtle use of barrel and stainless steel fermentation, oak aging, and other winemaking techniques to bring out the best in the fruit. All this is in keeping with his philosophy to allow the grapes from each vineyard to express their individual character in the final bottled wine.*

# POTATO &
# SORREL SOUP

*The sorrel lends the potato soup
not only its fresh green color,
but also its tangy flavor.*

2 tablespoons butter

2 tablespoons olive oil

1 onion, chopped

1$^{1}/2$ pounds potatoes, peeled and cut
into $^{1}/2$-inch cubes

2 cups chicken stock

1 cup Rodney Strong Vineyards Chardonnay

1 cup chopped lightly packed sorrel

$^{1}/2$ cup sour cream

1$^{1}/2$ teaspoons salt

1 teaspoon freshly ground black pepper

In a large pot, melt butter and olive oil over
medium heat. Add onion and sauté until tender.
Add potatoes, chicken stock, and wine. Cover and
simmer until potatoes are tender but not mushy.
Stir in sorrel, sour cream, salt, and pepper. Heat
through but do not let boil.

*Serves 4*
*Serve with Rodney Strong Vineyards*
*Chardonnay*

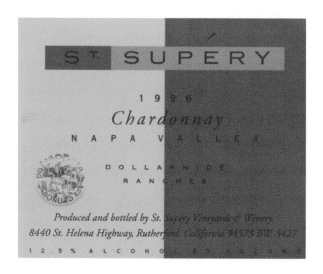

ST. SUPÉRY
1 9 9 6
*Chardonnay*
NAPA VALLEY
DOLLARHIDE
RANCHES

Produced and bottled by St. Supéry Vineyards & Winery,
8440 St. Helena Highway, Rutherford, California 94573 BW 5427
12.5% ALCOHOL BY VOLUME

## ST. SUPÉRY VINEYARDS AND WINERY

*No visit to the Napa Valley would be complete without a visit to the St. Supéry Wine Discovery Center in Rutherford. A demonstration vineyard, galleries within the center filled with panoramic murals, and displays all illustrate the lore of the vine. Both self-guided and guided tours serve to introduce the visitor to the wines and philosophy of St. Supéry.*

# SPICY SQUASH SOUP
## *with Ginger*

*As autumn approaches, you'll love a big bowl
of scrumptious seasonal soup. Ginger and
toasted spices make this traditional soup from
Sunny Cristadoro even more flavorful.*

1 large butternut squash

1 red bell pepper, cut in half and seeded

4 carrots, peeled and sliced

1 teaspoon cumin seed

1 teaspoon oregano

2 teaspoons peanut oil

1 small onion, chopped

1 tablespoon minced fresh ginger

1/4 cup St. Supéry Vineyards and
    Winery Chardonnay

4 cups chicken stock

Salt and freshly ground black pepper

1 tablespoon minced chives

*(recipe continued on next page)*

🍂 Preheat oven to 375° F. Lightly oil a roasting pan. Cut the squash in half lengthwise and scoop out the seeds. Place squash, flesh-side-down, in prepared roasting pan. Add about $1/2$-inch of water to the roasting pan. Roast 45 to 60 minutes, or until squash is very tender. Remove from oven and let cool. Scoop out flesh, chop coarsely, and set aside.

Place bell pepper on a baking sheet and roast along with the squash for about 30 minutes, or until charred all over. Remove from oven and immediately place in a bowl and cover with plastic wrap. When cool enough to handle, remove skin and chop the flesh. Set aside.

Place carrots in a steamer basket and steam until very tender. Set aside.

In a small sauté pan, toast the cumin seeds over medium heat until they start to pop. Add the oregano and stir until fragrant. Remove from heat and grind in a mortar and pestle until smooth. Set aside.

In a large pot, heat peanut oil over medium heat. Add onion and ginger and sauté until tender. Add the wine and simmer until liquid is reduced by half. Add the reserved squash, bell pepper, carrots,

*Who does not love wine,*
*women, and song, remains*
*a fool his whole life long.*

**Voss**

cumin, oregano, and chicken stock. Simmer over
low heat until heated through. Purée until smooth
and return to heat. Season with salt and pepper.
Serve with a sprinkling of chives.

*Serves 8*
*Serve with St. Supéry Vineyards and Winery*
*Chardonnay*

## NAVARRO VINEYARDS

*There are few wineries in northern California that have had the success with their wines that Navarro Vineyards has experienced. Visitors to this winery's tasting room, when asking about one of the current vintages, are often sorrowfully informed, "Sorry, the Chardonnay and Pinot Noir have sold out." This speaks to the absolute quality standards that Ted Bennet and Deborah Cahn have set for the wines they make. Known for their incredible delicacy and fruit, Navarro's wines are not just your standard California varietals. In addition to their outstanding Pinot Noir and Chardonnay, they take great pains to keep other, lesser-known wines in production. Their Chenin Blanc, White Riesling, and Gewürztraminers are known to wine lovers as among the world's finest, and their Sauvignon Blanc, Pinot Gris, Muscat Blanc, and Valdiguié never fail to charm first-time tasters.*

# PROVENÇAL FISH STEW *with Aioli*

*Serve with lots of crusty bread
to sop up the flavorful broth.*

## AIOLI:
4 cloves garlic, minced

2 egg yolks

$^1/_2$ cup olive oil

$^1/_2$ teaspoon salt

$^1/_2$ teaspoon white wine vinegar

## PROVENCAL FISH STEW:
$^1/_4$ cup olive oil

2 red bell peppers, seeded and chopped

1 onion, chopped

2 cloves garlic, minced

2 cups bottled clam juice

$1^1/_2$ cups Navarro Vineyards Sauvignon Blanc

4 tomatoes, peeled, seeded, and chopped

1 small serrano chile, seeded and minced

2 tablespoons minced fresh parsley

$^1/_2$ teaspoon oregano

$^1/_2$ teaspoon rosemary

$^1/_2$ teaspoon thyme

1 teaspoon salt

$^1/_2$ teaspoon freshly ground black pepper

6 (5-ounce) fish fillets, such as cod or sea bass

*(recipe continued on next page)*    **103**

**For the aioli:** Place the garlic and egg yolks in a blender and blend to mix. With the motor running, add the olive oil in a thin stream until all is incorporated and mixture is thick. Whisk in salt and vinegar. Transfer to a serving bowl, cover, and chill.

**For the stew:** In a large pot, heat olive oil over medium heat. Add bell peppers and onion and sauté about 10 minutes, or until tender. Add garlic and sauté until fragrant. Stir in clam juice and wine. Stir in tomatoes, chile, parsley, oregano, rosemary, thyme, salt, and pepper. Simmer, stirring often, for about 20 minutes or until slightly thickened.

Reduce heat to medium-low. Carefully slip fish fillets into the broth and simmer gently until fish is cooked. To serve, divide broth into six shallow bowls. Top with a fish fillet and a dollop of aioli. Pass remaining aioli at the table.

*Serves 6*
*Serve with Navarro Vineyards*
*Sauvignon Blanc*

## DRY CREEK VINEYARD

*Dry Creek Vineyard was the first new winery to be established in the Dry Creek Valley of Sonoma after Prohibition. Synonymous with fine winemaking, Dry Creek Vineyard draws upon over thirty-five different vineyards to produce their wines, matching the particular soils and microclimates of each site to the varieties that do best.*

# FUMÉ OYSTER CHOWDER

*For an elegant presentation, garnish with garlic croutons.*

1/2 cup butter

1 large onion, finely chopped

5 cloves garlic, minced

2 tablespoons all-purpose flour

1/2 cup Dry Creek Vineyard Fumé Blanc

4 cups milk

2 large potatoes, peeled and diced into 1/4-inch cubes

1/2 cup lightly packed parsley leaves, minced

2 teaspoons salt

1 teaspoon paprika

1 teaspoon white pepper

1 teaspoon Tabasco sauce

2 (10-ounce) jars extra-small oysters and their liquid

In a large pot, melt the butter over medium heat. Add onions and garlic and sauté until translucent. Sprinkle flour over onion mixture and whisk until smooth. Whisk in wine and simmer, whisking constantly, until almost all liquid has evaporated. Whisk in milk and bring to a simmer, whisking constantly. Stir in potatoes, parsley, salt, paprika, white pepper, and Tabasco sauce. Reduce heat to medium-low and simmer, stirring often, until potatoes are tender. Add oysters and simmer, stirring gently, for 5 to 10 minutes or until oysters are cooked and chowder has thickened.

*Serves 8*
*Serve with Dry Creek Vineyard*
*Fumé Blanc*

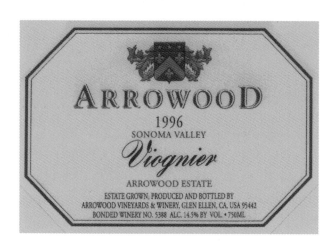

## ARROWOOD VINEYARDS
## AND WINERY

*Richard Arrowood, one of California's most renowned winemakers, and his wife and partner Alis Demers Arrowood, have crafted a winery that sits in perfect harmony with its environs. Fashioned after a New England farmhouse, the winery has often been described as a "winemaker's dream." Home to a number of wonderful, rare, and outstanding wines, Arrowood uses an intimate knowledge of the Sonoma Valley's many microclimates and terroirs to create great and complex wines.*

# LOBSTER & CORN CHOWDER

*This lobster and corn chowder is great
when you've been outside in the winter cold
all day and need a warmer-upper.*

1/4 cup butter

1 onion, finely chopped

1 carrot, finely chopped

1 stalk celery, finely chopped

1/2 teaspoon minced fresh thyme

1 tablespoon all-purpose flour

3 cups lobster stock or clam juice

1 cup heavy cream

2 cups corn kernels
    (from about 3 ears of corn)

1 potato, peeled and cut into
    1/4-inch cubes

1 pound cooked lobster meat,
    cut into 1/2-inch cubes

1 teaspoon salt

1/2 teaspoon freshly ground black pepper

*(recipe continued on next page)*

🦋 In a large pot, melt butter over medium heat. Add onion, carrot, celery, and thyme and sauté until just tender. Sprinkle flour over the vegetables and whisk until absorbed. Slowly whisk in stock. Reduce heat to low and simmer for 10 minutes, stirring constantly. Add the cream and increase heat to medium-low. Stir in corn and potato and simmer until potato is tender. Stir in lobster, salt, and pepper and heat through.

*Serves 6*
*Serve with Arrowood Vineyards and Winery*
*Viognier*

*A true German can't stand the French, yet willingly he drinks their wines.*

**Goethe**

CHARDONNAY
SONOMA COUNTY

ALC. 13.5% BY VOL.

# GEYSER PEAK WINERY

*Located just north of Healdsburg, 100-year-old Geyser Peak Winery's tradition of excellence shows in their being named "1998 Winery of the Year" by* Wine & Spirits *magazine and the San Francisco International Wine Competition. Their original vine-covered stone winery is now the cornerstone of a state-of-the-art complex that is one of the most well-equipped wineries in California. Within the winery, president and head winemaker Daryl Groom oversees the vinification of not only their sought-after reserve wines, but also a multitude of great wines for all occasions.*

# SMOKED SALMON
# & CORN CHOWDER

*If you live within driving distance of the coast of
California, make sure you pick up some locally
smoked salmon for this dish. Otherwise, pay
a visit to your local specialty foods counter for
this quintessential coastal delicacy.*

6 ounces bacon, diced

1/2 cup butter

2 onions, chopped

2 stalks celery, chopped

2 cloves garlic, minced

1 teaspoon paprika

1 teaspoon tarragon

3 tablespoons all-purpose flour

7 cups milk

4 1/2 cups diced potato, cut into 1/4-inch cubes

2 cups corn kernels

8 ounces smoked salmon, chopped

2 teaspoons freshly squeezed lemon juice

2 teaspoons freshly ground black pepper

2 teaspoons salt

In a large pot, sauté bacon over medium heat until crisp. Pour off excess fat. Add butter and increase heat to medium-high. Add onions, celery, and garlic and sauté until tender. Add paprika and tarragon. Sprinkle flour over onion mixture and stir with a whisk until flour is absorbed. Slowly whisk in 1 cup of the milk until blended. Whisk in remaining milk. Stir in potatoes, corn, smoked salmon, lemon juice, pepper, and salt. Bring chowder just to a boil, stirring constantly, then reduce heat to low and simmer until potatoes are tender and chowder is thick.

*Serves 8*
*Serve with Geyser Peak*
*Chardonnay*

## FETZER VINEYARDS

*"Live right, Eat right, Pick the right grapes"™ signifies the Fetzer Vineyards philosophy toward wine production and living in general. Fetzer has dedicated itself to being an environmentally and socially conscious grower, producer, and marketer of wines of the highest quality, and, to that end, farms 360 acres of certified organic grapes. Their award-winning wines run the gamut from Johannisberg Riesling to reserve Cabernet Sauvignon. Based in Mendocino County, Fetzer is one of the north coast's finest producers of premium wine.*

# POBLANO & SMOKED CHICKEN CHOWDER *with Hominy*

*John Ash sent this hearty and unusual soup recipe from his book,* From the Earth to the Table.

2 tablespoons olive oil

3 fresh poblano chiles, seeded and sliced into thin strips

2 onions, chopped

1 tablespoon minced garlic

6 cups rich chicken stock

2 cups fruity white wine such as Gewürztraminer or Riesling

2 cups husked and quartered tomatillos

1 1/2 cups chopped tomatoes

2 teaspoons oregano

1/2 teaspoon whole cumin seed

1/2 teaspoon whole fennel seed

1/4 teaspoon cinnamon

8 ounces smoked chicken, thinly sliced

3/4 cup cooked and drained white hominy

Salt and freshly ground black pepper

Diced avocado, chopped cilantro, and lime wedges, for garnish

*(recipe continued on next page)*

In a large pot, heat olive oil over medium-high heat. Add poblanos, onions, and garlic and sauté until tender but not brown. Stir in chicken stock, wine, tomatillos, tomatoes, oregano, cumin, fennel, and cinnamon and simmer for about 30 minutes. Add the chicken and hominy and heat through. Season with salt and pepper. Ladle into warm bowls and garnish with avocado, cilantro, and lime wedges.

*Serves 8 to 10*
*Serve with Fetzer Vineyards*
*Johannisberg Riesling*

*Wel loved he garleek, onyons*
*and lekes, and for to drynken*
*strong wyn, reed as blood.*

**Chaucer**

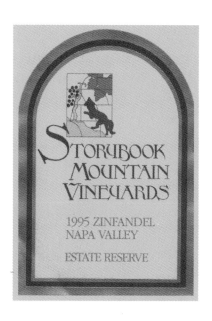

## STORYBOOK MOUNTAIN VINEYARDS

*At the extreme northern end of the Napa Valley lies Storybook Mountain Vineyards. Storybook Mountain is totally dedicated to Zinfandel and has established a worldwide reputation for consistently high quality. Proprietors Jerry and Sigrid Seps age their Zinfandel a minimum of twelve months inside century-old caves dug deep into the volcanic rock underlying their vineyards. Their wines are famed for their elegance and longevity. Notes of raspberries, black cherries, and spice are the keynote of these complex, well-balanced wines.*

# HUNGARIAN GOULASH SOUP

*This is the best way to warm up after those cold winter chores. Serve with a loaf of hot country bread in front of a warm fire.*

8 ounces lean pork, cut into $^1/_2$-inch cubes

4 ounces bacon, chopped

1 pound tomatoes, peeled, seeded, and chopped

2 onions, finely chopped

3 carrots, finely chopped

3 cloves garlic, minced

2 bay leaves

$^1/_2$ teaspoon caraway seeds

$^1/_2$ teaspoon thyme

$^1/_4$ teaspoon cayenne

$^1/_4$ teaspoon cumin

1 cup boiling water

1 cup Storybook Mountain Zinfandel

1 tablespoon hot paprika

1 tablespoon sweet paprika

1 cup sour cream

Zest of 1 lemon, finely minced

1/2 teaspoon sugar

Salt and freshly ground black pepper

In a large pot, combine pork and bacon. Sauté over medium heat until lightly browned. Drain off excess fat. Stir in tomatoes, onions, carrots, garlic, bay leaves, caraway, thyme, cayenne, and cumin. Reduce heat to medium-low, cover, and simmer for 30 minutes, stirring occasionally. Stir in water, wine, hot paprika, and sweet paprika and simmer 10 minutes. Stir in sour cream, lemon zest, and sugar and heat through but do not let boil. Season with salt and pepper to taste.

*Serves 4*
*Serve with Storybook Mountain*
*Zinfandel*

# THE WINERIES:

Alderbrook Winery
2306 Magnolia Drive
Healdsburg, CA 95448
707.433.9154

Arrowood Vineyards & Winery
14347 Sonoma Highway
Glen Ellen, CA 95442
707.938.5170

Belvedere Winery
435 West Dry Creek Road
Healdsburg, CA 95448
707.433.8236

Beringer Vineyards
2000 Main Street
St. Helena, CA 94574
707.963.7115

Cakebread Cellars
8300 St. Helena Highway
Rutherford, CA 94573
707.963.5221

Cardinale
Post Office Box 328
Oakville, CA 94562
707.944.2807

De Loach Vineyards
1791 Olivet Road
Santa Rosa, CA 95401
707.526.9111

Domaine Carneros
1240 Duhig Road
Napa, CA 94559
707.257.3020

Domaine Charbay Winery
4001 Spring Mountain Road
St. Helena, CA 94574
707.963.9327

Dry Creek Vineyard
3770 Lambert Bridge Road
Healdsburg, CA 95448
707.433.1000

Fetzer Vineyards
13601 Eastside Road
Hopland, CA 95449
707.744.7600

Flora Springs
1978 W. Zinfandel Lane
St. Helena, CA 94574
707.963.5711

Frey Vineyards
14000 Tomki Road
Redwood Valley, CA 95470
707.485.5177

Frog's Leap
8815 Conn Creek Road
Rutherford, CA 94573
707.963.4704

Geyser Peak Winery
22281 Chianti Road
Geyserville, CA 95441
707.857.9463

Gloria Ferrer Champagne Caves
23555 Highway 121
Sonoma, CA 95476
707.996.7256

Handley Cellars
3151 Highway 128
Philo, CA 95466
707.895.3876

Hess Collection Winery
4411 Redwood Road
Napa, CA 94558
707.255.1144

Hop Kiln Winery
6050 Westside Road
Healdsburg, CA 95448
707.433.6491

Husch Vineyards
4400 Highway 128
Philo, CA 95466
707.462.5370

Iron Horse Vineyards
9786 Ross Station Road
Sebastopol, CA 95472
707.887.1337

Kendall-Jackson Wine Center
5007 Fulton Road
Santa Rosa, CA 95439
707.571.8100

Kenwood Vineyards
9592 Sonoma Highway
Kenwood, CA 95452
707.833.5891

Korbel Champagne Cellars
13250 River Road
Guerneville, CA 95446
707.824.7000

Mont St. John Cellars
5400 Old Sonoma Road
Napa, CA 94558
707.255.8864

Navarro Vineyards
5601 Hwy 128
Philo, CA 95466
707.895.3686

Robert Mondavi Winery
7801 St. Helena Highway
Oakville, CA 94562
707.226.1395

Rodney Strong Vineyards
11455 Old Redwood Highway
Healdsburg, CA 95448
707.433.6521

Sebastiani Vineyards
389 Fourth Street, East
Sonoma, CA 95476
707.938.5532

Shafer Vineyards
6154 Silverado Trail
Napa, CA 94558
707.944.9454

St. Supéry Vineyards and Winery
8440 St. Helena highway
Rutherford, CA 94573
707.963.4507

Stonegate Winery
183 Dunaweal Lane
Calistoga, CA 94515
707.942.6500

Storybook Mountain Vineyards
3835 Highway 128
Calistoga, CA 94515
707.942.5310

Sutter Home Winery
100 St. Helena Highway, South
St. Helena, CA 94574
707.963.3104

Toad Hollow Vineyards
4024 West Side Road
Healdsburg, CA 95448
707.431.1441

Topolos Russian River Vineyards
5700 Gravenstein Highway, North
Forestville, CA 95436
707.887.1575

Trefethen Vineyards
1160 Oak Knoll Avenue
Napa, CA 94558
707.255.7700

Turnbull Wine Cellars
8210 St. Helena Highway
Oakville, CA 94562
800.887.6285

V. Sattui Winery
1111 White Lane
St. Helena, CA 94574
707.963.7774

Viansa Winery
25200 Arnold Drive
Sonoma, CA 95476
707.935.4700

Wente Estate Winery
5565 Tesla Road
Livermore, CA 94550
925.456.2300

## RESTAURANTS:

Chaminade at Santa Cruz
One Chaminade Lane
Santa Cruz, CA 95063
408.475.5600

Vinga Restaurant
320 3rd Street
San Francisco, CA 94107
415.546.3131

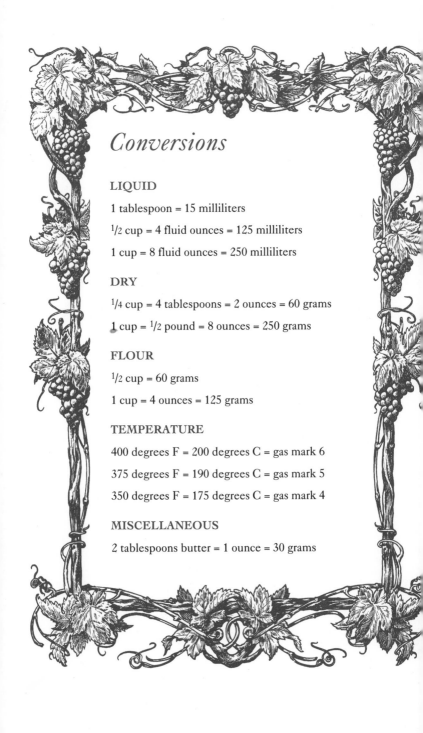

# *Conversions*

## LIQUID

1 tablespoon = 15 milliliters

1/2 cup = 4 fluid ounces = 125 milliliters

1 cup = 8 fluid ounces = 250 milliliters

## DRY

1/4 cup = 4 tablespoons = 2 ounces = 60 grams

1 cup = 1/2 pound = 8 ounces = 250 grams

## FLOUR

1/2 cup = 60 grams

1 cup = 4 ounces = 125 grams

## TEMPERATURE

400 degrees F = 200 degrees C = gas mark 6

375 degrees F = 190 degrees C = gas mark 5

350 degrees F = 175 degrees C = gas mark 4

## MISCELLANEOUS

2 tablespoons butter = 1 ounce = 30 grams